JUNK DRAWER
JEWELRY

Written by Rachel Di Salle and Ellen Warwick
Illustrated by Jane Kurisu

KIDS CAN PRESS

To Nadia, who can always make a silk purse out of a sow's ear.

Text © 2006 Rachel Di Salle and Ellen Warwick
Illustrations © 2006 Jane Kurisu

KIDS CAN DO IT® and the 🐾® logo are trademarks of Kids Can Press Ltd.

Kids Can Press acknowledges the financial support of the Government of Ontario, through the Ontario Media Development Corporation's Ontario Book Initiative, and the Government of Canada, through the BPIDP, for our publishing activity.

Published in Canada by
Kids Can Press Ltd.
29 Birch Avenue
Toronto, ON M4V 1E2

Published in the U.S. by
Kids Can Press Ltd.
2250 Military Road
Tonawanda, NY 14150

www.kidscanpress.com

Edited by Laurie Wark
Designed by Kathleen Collett
Photography by Ray Boudreau
Printed and bound in China

The hardcover edition of this book is smyth sewn casebound.
The paperback edition of this book is limp sewn with a drawn-on cover.

CM 06 0 9 8 7 6 5 4 3 2 1
CM PA 06 0 9 8 7 6 5 4 3 2 1

National Library of Canada Cataloguing in Publication Data

Di Salle, Rachel, 1976–
Junk drawer jewelry / written by Rachel Di Salle and Ellen Warwick ;
illustrated by Jane Kurisu.

(Kids can do it)

ISBN-13: 978-1-55337-965-2 (bound) ISBN-13: 978-1-55337-966-9 (pbk.)
ISBN-10: 1-55337-965-9 (bound) ISBN-10: 1-55337-966-7 (pbk.)

1. Jewelry making—Juvenile literature. 2. Handicraft—Juvenile literature.

I. Kurisu, Jane II. Warwick, Ellen III. Title. IV. Series.

TT212.D58 2006   j745.594'2   C2005-907888-X

Kids Can Press is a ʕ๏ɾႮs™ Entertainment company

Contents

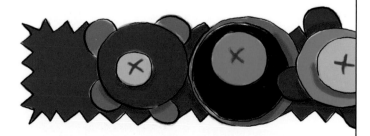

Introduction

Want to make super-cool jewelry without breaking the bank? How about spending a little time instead of a lot of money? Skip the mall and start digging around in the junk drawer, garage, toolbox or sewing kit. And you never know what treasures you could rescue from the recycling bins. You'll be amazed at the materials you can find that are already in your own home! If you don't find everything you need there, your next stop is the hardware store. It's not just for builders anymore! Think outside the (tool)box. Stroll through the aisles and check out all the nifty bits and pieces you can use to build your own personal style. After that, pop by your local music store and then on to the craft supply or fabric store. Keep your crafty eyes peeled wherever you go, and you'll find inspiration in the most unlikely places.

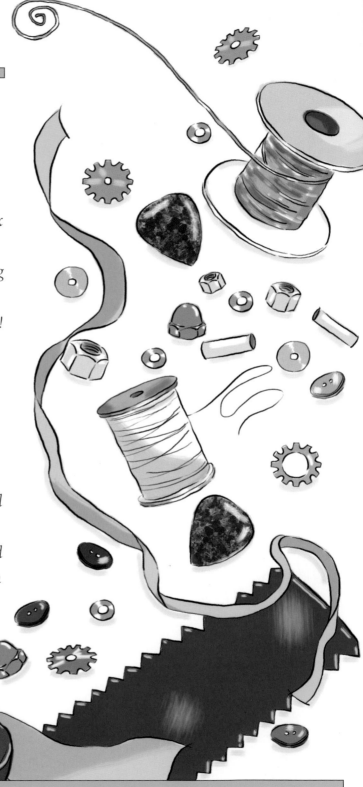

GETTING STARTED

Before you dive into your first project, check out this section for tips, tricks and not-to-be-missed safety information. Make sure to protect your work surface with a cutting mat, newspaper or a piece of cardboard. And don't forget to protect yourself! Always wear safety goggles and work gloves when hammering, cutting or bending wire, or using a glue gun.

❈ Safety is #1 with the glue gun

There are two types of glue guns: low temperature and high temperature. The low temperature kind is safest to use, but the glue won't always stick as well as with the high temperature kind. Be sure to have an adult give you a hand.

❈ Eyelets are exciting

Eyelets have two pieces, a barrel and a washer. You'll need an eyelet tool, which also has two pieces: a stud tool and a base tool. Make sure you work on a hard surface, such as a workbench, a basement floor or a flat brick. Read the package directions and always have an adult handy to help out.

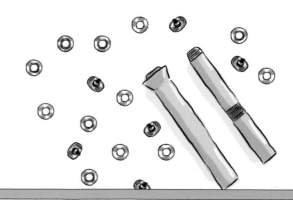

✿ Pliers and wire cutters

For most projects, a small pair of needlenose pliers with side cutters will get the job done. The pointy ends are great for bending wire and picking up small beads. The side cutters can cut thin wire, small chain, head pins and eye pins. Use wire cutters for heavier wire and chain.

You'll also need roundnose pliers. They are great for bending wire into perfectly shaped loops. To make a loop, hold the wire or pin in one hand and use the pliers to grasp the wire about 0.5 cm (1/4 in.) from the end. Bend the wire to make an L shape, then grasp the tip of the wire and twist it into a small circle.

✿ What's shrinkable plastic?

This really cool plastic shrinks to one-quarter of its original size when it's put in a hot oven. Be sure to read the manufacturer's instructions before you begin. Ask an adult to help you with the oven and remember to wear oven mitts when handling anything hot. Allow the pan and the plastic to cool completely before touching them with your bare hands.

❀ Jewelry findings

Clasps: Most of the crafts in this book use spring rings or lobster clasps for closures, but you can use whatever kind you like.

Jump rings: These small round rings are used to link things together. To open them, gently separate the overlapped ends with pliers. To close them, ply the ends together to form a loop.

Head pins and eye pins: A head pin looks like a sewing pin without a sharp end. An eye pin has a loop at the top instead of a head. Both can be bent into loops or other shapes.

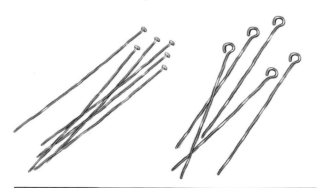

Ring forms: These rings have a flat circular or oval piece on top that you can glue any object to.

Earring wires: Attach a bauble to the looped end of an earring wire and slip the other end through a pierced ear.

Ribbon closures: Slide them onto the end of your necklace or bracelet when using ribbon, fabric or other flat material. Use pliers to pinch them shut.

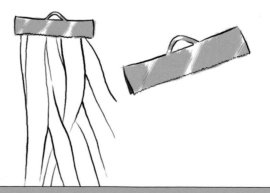

Lace-it-up leather bracelet

Weave a wickedly cool bracelet with leather cord and beads. For an awesome belt, make a bracelet that's long enough to fit around your waist or hips.

YOU WILL NEED

- 4 pieces of leather cord, each 90 cm (36 in.) long
- about 100 plastic pony beads
- masking tape, scissors

1 Fold one cord in half and tie a knot near the folded end, leaving a 1 cm (1/2 in.) loop. Repeat with the other three cords.

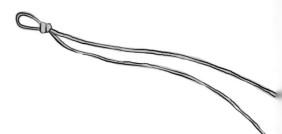

2 Lay the cords close together with the knots lined up. Use masking tape to stick the cords to the work surface.

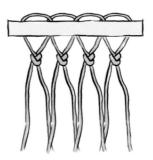

3 String one bead onto the two ends of each folded cord and slide them up close to the knots. This row has four beads.

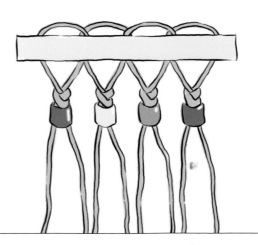

4 Starting at the right side, string a bead onto the first cord. Then string a bead onto the next two cords together, another bead onto the next two cords, then the next two again, and finally one bead onto the last cord. Slide the beads up against the first row of beads. This row has five beads.

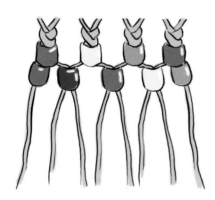

5 Repeat steps 3 and 4 until the bracelet is long enough to fit around your wrist. Finish with a row of four beads.

6 Tie a knot close to each bead and trim each of the cord ends to 8 cm (3 in.). Remove the tape.

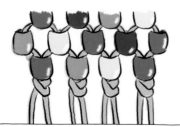

7 String a bead onto four of the cord ends on one side. Fold the bracelet in half and push the four cord ends through two of the loops at the top of the bracelet. Add another bead onto the four cord ends. Repeat this step with the remaining four cord ends.

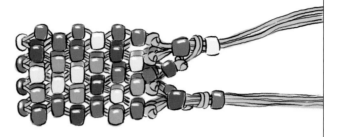

8 Add one bead onto each of the cord ends and tie a knot at the end of each cord.

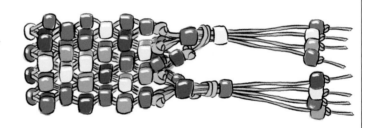

9 Slide the beads from step 7 toward the end of the cords to widen the bracelet. Slide the bracelet onto your wrist, then slide the beads back to tighten it.

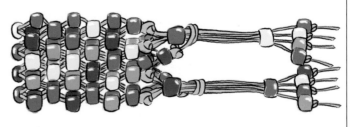

Totally tubular necklace

You'll clearly be cool when you tie on this totally topped-up necklace.

YOU WILL NEED

- 0.5 m (1/2 yd.) of 0.5 cm x 0.43 cm (1/4 in. x 3/16 in.) clear vinyl tubing
- 2 red ring terminals, wire range 22–16 and stud size 4–6 (available at hardware stores)
- a small envelope
- round rainbow-colored cake decorations
- 2 pieces of 0.25 cm (1/8 in.) ribbon, each 50 cm (20 in.) long
- a measuring tape, scissors

1 Measure around your neck and add 5 cm (2 in.). Cut the tubing to this length.

2 Holding the metal end, push a ring terminal 0.5 cm (1/4 in.) into one end of the tube.

3 Cut the envelope about 0.25 cm (1/8 in.) across one bottom corner to make a funnel.

4 Holding the cut corner of the envelope closed, pour some cake decorations in and tuck the flap inside.

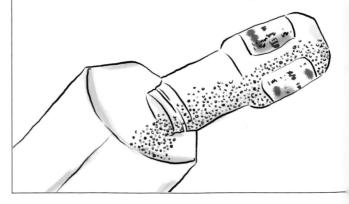

5 Pour the cake decorations into the tube. Leave about 1 cm (1/2 in.) of space at the top of the tube.

6 Repeat step 2 to put a ring terminal into the other end of the tube.

7 Fold one piece of ribbon in half and push this folded end through the metal hole in one ring terminal to make a loop. Draw the ends of the ribbon through the loop and make a knot close to the ring terminal.

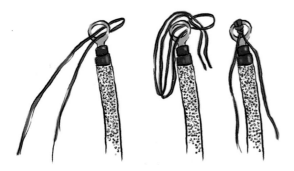

8 Repeat step 7 to add a ribbon to the other ring terminal. Put the necklace around your neck and tie a bow to secure it.

OTHER IDEAS

Make it stripy with layers of colored sand, or glitzy with glitter, or hard-core with tiny metal ball bearings. Use your imagination to think of other neat-o little bits to fit inside the tube for a look that suits your style.

Super-stacked washer ring

Loads of layers make for an edgy, modern ring.

YOU WILL NEED

- a ring form
- a 0.5 cm (1/4 in.) flat brass washer
- a 6 mm (1/4 in.) flat stainless steel washer
- a 0.4 cm (5/32 in.) flat brass washer
- a 0.5 cm (1/4 in.) 4-40 machine screw nut
- a 0.5 cm (1/4 in.) external-tooth washer
- a bead
- a 2.5 cm (1 in.) head pin
- either an egg carton, a small box or a small piece of foam
- a glue gun, scissors, needlenose pliers with side cutters

1 Cut a small slit into either the egg carton, the box or the foam. Slide the ring form into the slit so that the flat part is facing up.

2 Using the glue gun, apply a bead of hot glue to the flat top of the ring form. Use the pliers to hold the 0.5 cm (1/4 in.) flat brass washer and gently press it into the glue. Make sure it is centered on the ring form.

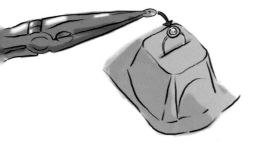

3 Apply another bead of glue and add the 6 mm (1/4 in.) flat stainless steel washer. Repeat with the 0.4 cm (5/32 in.) flat brass washer, the 0.5 cm (1/4 in.) 4-40 machine screw nut, and the 0.5 cm (1/4 in.) external tooth washer. Allow the glue to dry.

4 With the side cutters of the pliers, trim 1.5 cm (5/8 in.) off the end of the head pin.

5 String the bead on the head pin and press the end of the pin down into the center of the ring.

6 Use scissors to trim off any excess glue around the edge of the ring.

OTHER IDEAS

Glue small bolts or washers to the ring form in a star or flower pattern. Then glue a bead or nut in the center.

Very vinyl wristband

This funky addition to your jewelry box could also be made from plastic, fabric or leather. To make a fashion statement that actually says something, replace some of the shapes with cut-out vinyl letters that spell a cool word or your initials.

YOU WILL NEED

- a piece of red vinyl that is about 43 cm (17 in.) x 5 cm (2 in.)
- small pieces of yellow, orange, turquoise and dark blue vinyl
- a small circle of peel-and-stick Velcro
- red thread
- a measuring tape, pinking shears, a pencil, tracing paper, scissors, a needle and a thimble

1 Measure around your wrist and add 2.5 cm (1 in.). With pinking shears, cut a piece of red vinyl this long and 2.5 cm (1 in.) wide.

2 Trace the shapes from page 40 onto tracing paper. Cut out the shapes.

3 Use the tracing-paper shapes to trace 21 shapes on different colors of vinyl. Cut them out with the scissors.

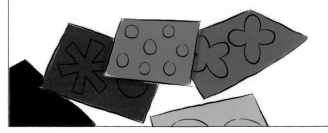

4 Experiment with the placement of the shapes to make seven groups of three shapes, each layered from biggest to smallest.

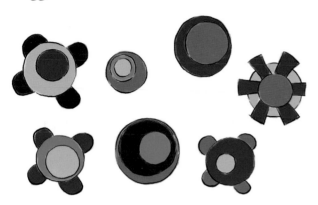

5 Cut a piece of thread about as long as your arm. Thread the needle so that the ends meet. Knot the ends together.

6 Lay one group of shapes at the end of the red band. Using the thimble, push the needle up through all the vinyl layers, close to the middle of the shapes. Push the needle back down about 0.5 cm (¹/₄ in.) over. Repeat this twice.

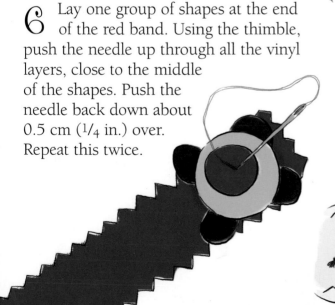

7 Push the needle back up and down to create an **X** and repeat this twice. Tie a knot on the underside and cut off the excess thread.

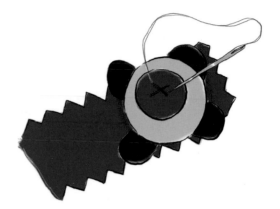

8 Repeat steps 6 and 7 for the rest of the shape groups, keeping them close together so that there is about 1 cm (¹/₂ in.) of band left at the end.

9 For a fastener, peel and stick one half of the Velcro circle onto the right (good) side at the end of the band. Stick the other half of the Velcro onto the wrong side at the other end of the band.

Eye-catching eyelet choker

Make an eye-popping, jaw-dropping choker with a little ribbon and some handy eyelets. Try velvet and silver ribbon with glass beads for a classy look.

YOU WILL NEED

- 0.5 m (¹/₂ yd.) blue grosgrain ribbon, 1.5 cm (⁵/₈ in.) wide
- 1/2 m (¹/₂ yd.) orange ribbon, 3 mm (¹/₈ in.) wide
- seven 8 mm (³/₈ in.) eyelets and a small eyelet tool
- 9 beads
- three 2.5 cm (1 in.) head pins
- 2 ribbon closures, 1.5 cm (⁵/₈ in.) wide
- 2 jump rings
- a clasp
- a measuring tape, scissors, a pencil, a hammer, needlenose pliers

1 Measure around your neck. Cut a piece of blue ribbon this length. Add 4 cm (1¹/₂ in.) to this measurement and cut a piece of orange ribbon this length.

2 With a pencil, mark the middle of the blue ribbon. Mark 3 cm (1¹/₄ in.) on each side of this mark and repeat twice adding 3 cm (1¹/₄ in.) each time so you have seven evenly spaced marks. Add an eyelet at each mark (see page 5).

3 String three beads onto a head pin and use the pliers to make a small open loop at the top of the pin. Repeat to make two more beaded head pins.

4 Lay the blue ribbon right (good) side down. Lay the orange ribbon on top, lining up the ribbons at one end. Using the pliers, add a ribbon closure to hold the ends together.

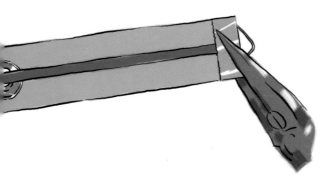

5 Starting at the closure end, thread the orange ribbon up through the first eyelet, and then down through the second eyelet.

6 Thread the ribbon up through the third eyelet and through the loop of a beaded head pin. Use the pliers to pinch the loop closed. String the ribbon back down through the third eyelet, leaving about 1 cm ($1/2$ in.) of ribbon to make a loop for the beaded head pin to hang from. Thread up through the sixth eyelet and down through the seventh.

7 Trim the orange ribbon so that it's the same length as the blue ribbon and add a ribbon closure using the pliers.

8 Add a jump ring to each ribbon closure and add a clasp to one of the jump rings (see page 7).

Seriously sequined earrings

*Go for glitz and glam and add some
pizzazz to an ordinary day.*

YOU WILL NEED

- fourteen 0.5 cm (¹/₄ in.) jump rings
- 26 sequins
- 2 earring wires
- needlenose pliers

1 Hold a jump ring on the end of the needlenose pliers. Pull one side of the jump ring towards you to make a 0.25 cm (¹/₈ in.) opening.

2 Add two sequins to each of the six open jump rings.

3 Attach an earring wire to one of the jump rings. Use the pliers to pinch the jump ring closed.

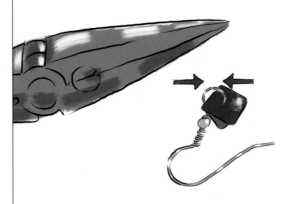

4 Attach a second jump ring to the first by slipping it between the two sequins and closing the jump ring.

5 Repeat step 4 to attach four more jump rings with sequins, each one below the last.

6 Open another jump ring and add one sequin to it. Slip it onto the bottom jump ring between the two sequins and close the jump ring.

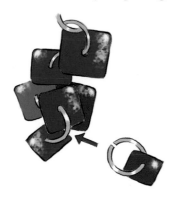

7 Repeat steps 1 to 6 to make a second earring.

OTHER IDEAS

Make a matching bracelet or necklace by linking enough sequined jump rings together to wrap around your wrist or neck. Add a clasp to one end to fasten it.

Hard-wear necklace

Take a trip to the hardware store or your family toolbox to make a necklace with heavy-duty style.

YOU WILL NEED

- 1 m (3 ft.) of 0.125 cm ($^1/_{16}$ in.) aircraft cable
- four 0.125 cm ($^1/_{16}$ in.) aluminum sleeves for cable (crimps)
- four 8 mm ($^3/_8$ in.) stainless steel machine screw nuts
- four 0.375 cm ($^1/_8$ in.) brass flat washers
- three 0.625 cm x 0.625 cm ($^3/_{16}$ in. x $^3/_{16}$ in.) brass hose barb splicers
- 2 brass acorn nuts
- two 0.625 cm ($^1/_4$ in.) stainless steel flat washers
- two 4-40 stainless steel machine screw nuts
- two 8 mm ($^3/_8$ in.) brass machine screw nuts
- two 0.375 cm ($^1/_8$ in.) stainless steel flat washers
- one 0.25 cm ($^1/_8$ in.) quick link
- a measuring tape, wire cutters, a small piece of wood, a hammer

1 Measure around your neck to the length you want the necklace to be and add 10 cm (4 in.). Using wire cutters, cut a piece of aircraft cable to this length.

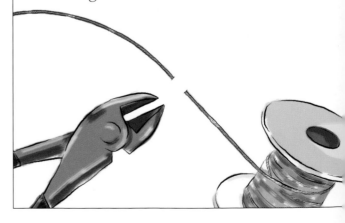

2 Slide a cable sleeve onto one end of the cable and then insert the cable back into the sleeve to make a small loop. Make sure the short end of the cable does not extend beyond the sleeve.

3 Lay the sleeve onto a piece of wood and hammer it a few times to hold the wire loop in place.

4 String the hardware pieces onto the cable, alternating the nuts, washers and hose barb splicers as shown or in any pattern you like.

5 Repeat steps 2 and 3 to create a wire loop at the other end of the cable.

6 Open the quick link and put one of the wire loops through the opening. Put the necklace around your neck. Hook the other loop through the quick link and screw it closed.

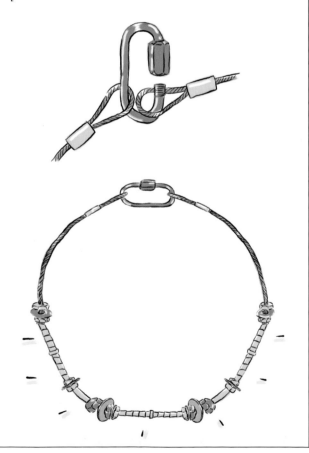

Orb-it ring

Use any picture you adore for this one-of-a-kind ring — a photo, a magazine clip, a postcard or your own artwork — as long as it's tiny enough to fit under a glass bead.

YOU WILL NEED

- a glass bead
- a very small picture or photo
- a ring form
- either an egg carton, a small box or a small piece of foam
- a pencil, scissors, white glue, a small paint brush, a glue gun

1 With the flat side down, place the glass bead on top of the picture and move it around until you like the way the picture looks through the bead.

2 Trace around the bead, holding it in place with your finger.

3 Cut out the picture just inside the line you traced so that it is slightly smaller than the bead.

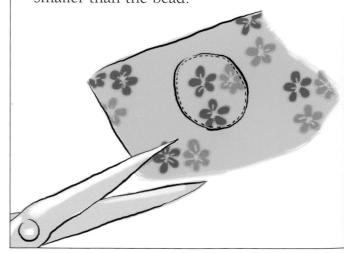

4 Paint a thick layer of white glue on the flat side of the bead. Stick the right (good) side of the picture onto the bead so that the picture shows through it.

5 Paint a thick layer of white glue over the back of the image and set it aside to dry. Repeat and allow to dry again.

6 Cut a small slit into either an egg carton, a small box or a small piece of foam. Slide the ring form into the slit so that the flat part is facing up.

7 Using the glue gun, apply a generous bead of glue to the top of the ring form and press the glass bead onto it with the picture on the bottom. Allow to dry.

ANOTHER IDEA

Stick one of the beads onto a small metal hair clip to make some hair jewelry.

Groovin' guitar pick necklace

Get in the groove and harmonize your style with this soul strummin' necklace. Guitar picks come in many colors, so pick your favorites and get stringing!

YOU WILL NEED

- 8 thin orange guitar picks
- 8 thin tortoise shell (brown) guitar picks
- 1 m (3 ft.) of brown satin cord
- clear nail polish
- a 0.25 cm (1/8 in.) single-hole punch, a ruler, scissors

1 Using the hole punch, make holes about 0.25 cm (1/8 in.) from the top and bottom of an orange guitar pick. Repeat with six more orange picks.

2 Make a hole about 0.25 cm (1/8 in.) from the bottom of a brown guitar pick. Make another hole in the middle of this pick. Repeat with six more brown picks.

3 Tie a knot in the cord 34 cm (13 1/2 in.) from one end. Thread the longer end of the cord up through the bottom hole of an orange guitar pick.

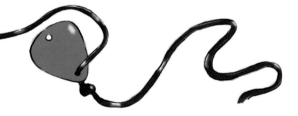

4 Place the top hole of the orange guitar pick under the bottom hole of a brown guitar pick. Thread the cord down through both holes.

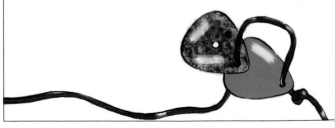

5 Place the middle hole of the brown guitar pick under the bottom hole of another orange guitar pick. Pull the cord up through both holes.

8 Punch a hole 0.25 cm (¹/₈ in.) from the top and bottom of the last two guitar picks. Thread one cord end up through one hole and down through another. Tie a knot leaving 2.5 cm (1 in.) of cord at the end. Repeat with the other cord and guitar pick.

6 Repeat steps 4 and 5 until you have used all of the hole-punched guitar picks. Tie a knot close to the last guitar pick, leaving about 38 cm (15 in.).

7 Take the longer end of the cord and loosely wrap it around the shorter end three times. Thread the longer end through the loops, starting with the first loop. Pull this knot tight. The shorter end should now slide easily through longer end so that you can adjust the necklace to the length you want.

9 Trim the ends of the cords and dab clear nail polish on the ends to prevent fraying.

Button bonanza bracelet

Raid your button jar to find jewels you never knew you had. Use any color scheme you like.

YOU WILL NEED

- 1 m (1 ft.) red organza or sheer ribbon, 0.5 cm (1/4 in.) wide
- 6 light blue and 6 dark blue buttons
- 8 red buttons
- 2 ribbon closures, 2 cm (3/4 in.) wide
- 2 jump rings
- a clasp
- a needle with a large eye for the ribbon to fit through
- a measuring tape, scissors, masking tape, needlenose pliers

1 Measure around your wrist and add 2.5 cm (1 in.). Cut six pieces of ribbon this length.

2 Thread the needle with one piece of ribbon. Push the needle up through a hole in a light blue button and back down through the other hole. String on two more light blue buttons this way, spacing them evenly apart. Leave about 4 cm (1 1/2 in.) of ribbon at each end. Repeat with another ribbon and the remaining three light blue buttons.

3 Repeat step 2 with two more ribbons and the dark blue buttons.

4 String four red buttons onto each of the last two ribbons, leaving 2.5 cm (1 in.) of ribbon at each end.

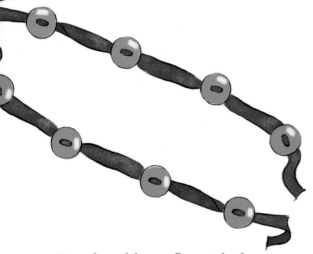

5 Lay the ribbons flat with the buttons facing up and the ends lined up evenly on one side. Stick them down with a piece of masking tape about 2.5 cm (1 in.) from the ends.

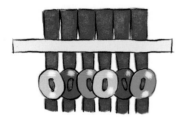

6 Tuck the ribbon ends into a ribbon closure. Using the pliers, gently close the closure, making sure the ribbon ends are inside. Remove the tape.

7 Repeat steps 5 and 6 to add a ribbon closure to the other side of the bracelet.

8 Using the pliers, open a jump ring (see page 7) and put the ring through the hole on the end of a ribbon closure. Add a clasp to the ring and close it with the pliers.

9 Add another jump ring to the other ribbon closure.

Superstar origami earrings

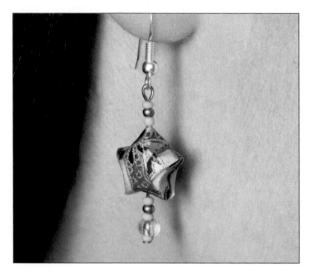

Show off your star power with these sure-to-make-you-famous earrings.

YOU WILL NEED

- a small piece of colorful paper, such as wrapping paper, origami paper or magazine clippings
- two 4 cm (1½ in.) head pins
- 14 seed beads
- 2 glass E beads
- 2 earring wires
- either an egg carton, a small cardboard box or a piece of foam
- a ruler, scissors, two sewing pins, a small paint brush
- white glue, roundnose or needlenose pliers

1 Cut out a strip of paper 14 cm x 1 cm (5½ in. x ½ in.).

2 Tie a loose knot at the end of the strip. Gently pull the knot tight and flatten it out to make a five-sided shape as shown. Trim the short end of the strip so it is even with the knot's side.

3 Wrap the long end of the strip around the knot, folding it along each side of the knot. Continue until there is about 2 cm (³⁄₄ in.) of the strip remaining. Tuck this end under one of the folds. Gently push in the middle of each of the shape's sides to make the star puff out.

4 Push a sewing pin through the star between two of its points and out the opposite point. Push the pin into either an egg carton, a small cardboard box or a piece of foam to hold it upright.

7 Add a seed bead, an E bead, and three more seed beads to a head pin. Push the pin through the holes in a star and add three more seed beads.

5 Repeat steps 1 to 4 to make a second star.

6 Mix a small, equal amount of glue and water in a dish. Using the paint brush, apply an even coat of glue mixture onto each star. Allow to dry, and then add two more coats. Allow the stars to dry overnight. Remove the pins.

8 Using the pliers, bend the top of the head pin to form a small loop. Hook an earring wire onto the loop and pinch it closed. Repeat steps 7 and 8 for the other earring.

Galaxy-girl charm bracelet

Blast off to interstellar style with a charm bracelet that's out of this world! Then make space-y charms and attach them to earring wires for awesome astro earrings.

YOU WILL NEED

- a package of opaque shrinkable plastic sheets
- 20 cm (8 in.) of colored chain with a gauge of 0.5 cm (¼ in.)
- jump rings
- a clasp
- a pencil, tracing paper, sandpaper, paper towel, permanent markers, a small paint brush, a sealer product such as Mod Podge or other acrylic varnish
- a 0.25 cm (⅛ in.) single-hole punch, scissors, measuring tape, needlenose pliers

1 Trace the outer-space templates from page 40 onto tracing paper.

2 Lightly sand one side of a sheet of shrinkable plastic, then wipe it with a paper towel.

3 Lay the sheet sanded-side up on the traced pictures. With a black marker, trace the pictures onto the plastic sheet. Color the images with markers.

4 Using the hole punch, make a hole about 0.5 cm (1/4 in.) above each picture. Cut around them, leaving about 0.5 cm (1/4 in.) of white space around the picture and the hole.

5 Have an adult help you shrink the charms in the oven, following the package directions. Allow to cool.

6 Using the paint brush, apply a thin layer of sealer onto the picture side of each charm. Allow to dry.

7 Measure around your wrist and add 2.5 cm (1 in.). Using the pliers, remove links to make the chain this length.

8 Open a jump ring with the pliers (see page 7) and put a charm onto the ring. Slip the ring through a link on the chain and use the pliers to close the ring. Repeat for all of the charms, spacing them evenly.

9 Add a jump ring to one end of the chain and close the ring. Open the link at the other end of the chain. Slip a clasp onto the link and close the link.

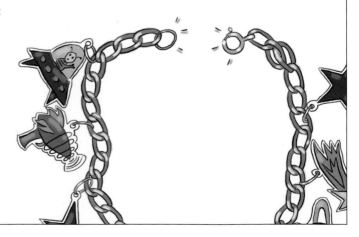

Wicked wire ring

Weave an awesome artsy ring with copper wire and glass beads.

YOU WILL NEED

- 60 cm (24 in.) of 20 gauge copper wire
- about 15 beads of different shapes, sizes and colors
- a measuring tape, 2 needlenose pliers with side cutters

1 Using the side cutters, cut the wire into one 40 cm (16 in.) piece and one 20 cm (8 in.) piece.

2 With a measuring tape, measure around your finger and add 1.5 cm ($^5/_8$ in.). Mark this length on the 40 cm (16 in.) wire. Gently bend the wire at the mark and make a small loop by twisting the end of the wire around once.

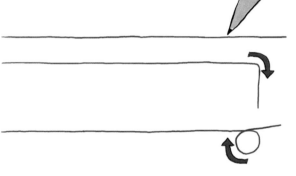

3 Holding the loop with needlenose pliers, wind the longer end of wire around the shorter end as shown. Keep the coils tight and close together.

4 Continue winding until there is 1.5 cm (5/8 in.) of the shorter wire left. Trim the longer wire to the same length as the short wire.

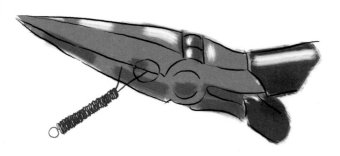

5 Bend the coiled wires around to make a circle. Push the wire ends through the small loop.

6 Wrap the wire ends around the outside of the loop twice, ending on the top edge of the ring. Trim any remaining wire ends.

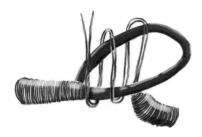

7 Push the 20 cm (8 in.) wire through the loop from step 2, so that the wire is even on both sides of the ring.

8 String a bead onto one end of the wire, fold the wire over and pull it through the ring opening. Pull the wire tight. Repeat with the other end of wire.

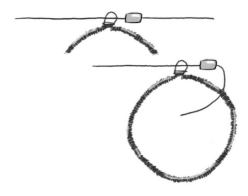

9 Continue adding beads and pulling the wire through the ring until you like the way it looks. Cut the wire ends leaving 0.5 cm (1/4 in.). Bend the wire ends and tuck them in so there are no sharp ends sticking out.

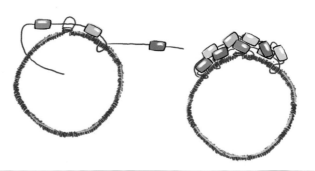

Eclectic electric bracelet

Electrify your style with a shockingly cool bracelet! Not a garden guru? Express your style with shapes that suit you to a tee — just make sure there's enough room to punch two holes in the middle.

1 Measure around your wrist and add 2.5 cm (1 in.). Cut a piece of wire in each color to this length.

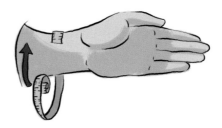

2 Trace the flower shape from page 40 onto tracing paper and cut it out. Use the shape to trace 15 flowers onto different colors of craft foam and then cut them out.

3 Using the hole punch, make two holes about 0.5 cm (1/4 in.) apart in the center of each flower shape.

4 Put a wire up through one flower hole and back down through the other hole. String two more flowers onto the wire this way. String three flowers onto each of the other four wires.

5 Line up the wire ends on one side. Stick them down with a piece of masking tape about 2.5 cm (1 in.) from the ends.

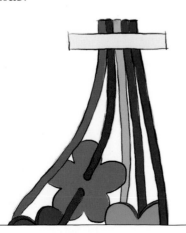

6 Tuck the wire ends into a ribbon closure. Close it with the pliers, making sure the wire ends are all inside. Remove the tape.

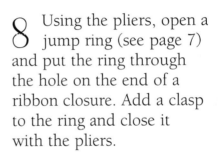

7 Repeat steps 5 and 6 to add a ribbon closure to the other end of the bracelet.

8 Using the pliers, open a jump ring (see page 7) and put the ring through the hole on the end of a ribbon closure. Add a clasp to the ring and close it with the pliers.

9 Add another jump ring to the other ribbon closure.

Bathing beauty bathtub-chain anklet

Make a splash with an anklet that's anything but wishy-washy. You can wear this everywhere — even in the tub!

YOU WILL NEED

- 50 cm (20 in.) of bathtub chain
- 2 bathtub-chain connectors
- a package of 22 mm (7/8 in.) eye pins
- assorted beads
- a measuring tape, roundnose or needlenose pliers with side cutters

1 Measure around your ankle and add 1 cm (1/2 in.). Using the wire cutters, cut two pieces of bathtub chain to this length.

2 Attach a connector to one end of each piece of chain.

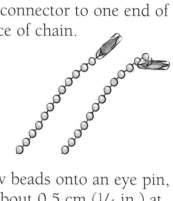

3 Slip a few beads onto an eye pin, leaving about 0.5 cm (1/4 in.) at the top of the eye pin free.

4 Using the pliers, bend the straight end of the eye pin to form a small loop that is the same size as the loop at the top.

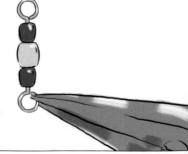

5 With the pliers, open one eye pin loop. Starting at the closure end of one chain, slip the loop between the first and second balls of the chain and close it with the pliers.

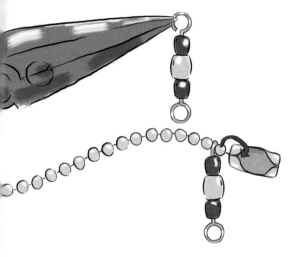

7 Starting at one end of the chain, open the loop on the other end of the beaded eye pin. Slip the loop onto the other chain at the same place as it is on the first chain. Close the loop.

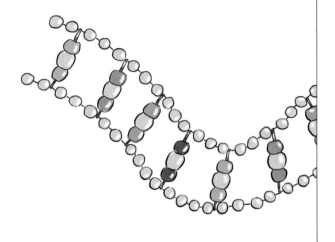

6 Repeat steps 3 and 4 to make another beaded eye pin. Repeat step 5 to attach it to the chain, leaving three balls between the first and second beaded eye pins. Continue adding a beaded eye pin for every three balls on the chain until you have at least two balls left at the end.

8 Repeat step 7 with the remaining beaded eye pins.

9 Wrap the anklet around your ankle and snap the chain ends into the connectors at the other sides of the links.

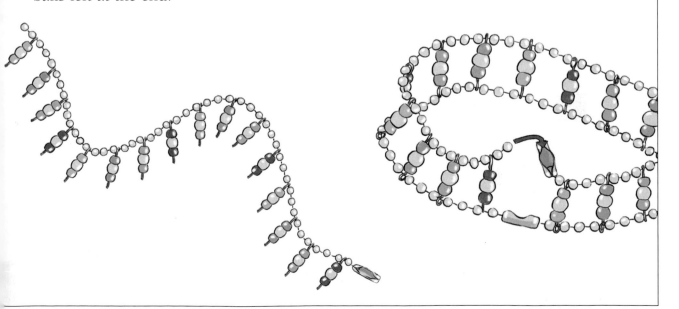

Daring duct tape wristband

Add some attitude to your next outfit with a simple yet oh-so-stylish wristband, complete with flashy silver eyelets.

YOU WILL NEED

- red and blue duct tape
- five 8 mm (3/8 in.) eyelets and a small eyelet tool
- a small square of peel-and-stick Velcro
- a measuring tape, scissors, pinking shears, a pencil

1 Measure around your wrist and add 4 cm (1 1/2 in.). Cut a piece of red duct tape this length.

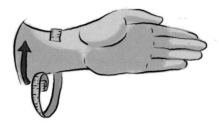

2 Lay the tape down with the sticky side up. Fold one long edge over by about one-third, pressing the sticky sides together. Fold it over again.

3 Cut a piece of blue duct tape the same length as the red piece. Lay the blue piece of duct tape down with the sticky side up.

4 With the seam side down, stick the red folded duct tape down the center of the blue duct tape.

5 Fold one edge of the blue duct tape over to meet the edge of the red duct tape. Repeat this step for the other blue duct tape edge.

6 Trim the ends of the wristband with pinking shears.

7 Measure and mark the center of the wristband. Make a mark 2 cm (3/4 in.) on each side of the center mark. Repeat 4 cm (1 1/2 in.) on each side of the center mark.

8 Add an eyelet at each mark (see page 5).

9 Peel and stick one Velcro piece about 1.5 cm (5/8 in.) from the inside edge of one end of the wristband. Stick the other Velcro piece about 1.5 cm (5/8 in.) from the outside edge of the other end of the wristband.

TEMPLATES

Very vinyl wristband (page 14)

Galaxy-girl charm bracelet (page 30)

Eclectic electric bracelet (page 34)

40